H A
time and
money by
managing
organisational
change
effectively

First edition published in Great Britain in 2003 by:
Go MAD Books
Pocket Gate Farm
Off Breakback Road
Woodhouse Eaves
Leicestershire
LE12 8RS

ISBN 0-9551287-6-5

British Library Cataloguing in Publication Data.
A catalogue record for this book is available from the British Library.

Printed in Great Britain by the MPG Books Group
Bodmin and King's Lynn

Go MAD® is a registered trademark.

Contents

"Progress is impossible without change;
and those who cannot change their minds
cannot change anything."
George Bernard Shaw

INTRODUCTION

The reason this book was originally written

Back in 1997 I realised that very few, if any, management and leadership programmes included pragmatic material about how to handle, manage and develop people through change. So, this book was originally written in 1998, and revised in 2003, to summarise the key points and essential information that I believe every manager should understand and apply when managing teams through change. It is largely based on the academic and case-study research of 67 organisations conducted by myself, about what has now become termed "Survivor Syndrome".

Time for a 3rd edition

Over 10 years on from its original publication the material is as relevant today as it was then, if not more so. In recent years, I have noticed that the demand for the book, and requests to use the Go MAD® Thinking System, is increasing as organisations realise that the business improvement methodologies that have become well known over the past decade – such as Lean and Six Sigma – don't always get the desired results. This is often because managing the people side of change is frequently overlooked and managers lack the confidence and skills to be able to do it.

Also, at around the same time as its first publication I conducted a major piece of research into the key success principles that people naturally apply when they make a difference. From this came the Go MAD® Thinking System: a framework that gives individuals and organisations a common language and toolkit to enable them to think in a solution focused way in order to achieve the results they want. A system that today is used by hundreds of thousands of people across the world to achieve the business differences they want to make.

Jo and I spend much of our time using the Go MAD® Thinking System to help people with their thinking during periods of organisational change and equipping them with the tools and skills to be able to do this. So, our purpose in creating a new edition of this book was to include the Go MAD® Thinking System for the first time. Many of our clients report that the Go MAD® Thinking System is the "glue" that binds everything together during change.

I know from my research that the quality of people's thinking is ignored or assumed in many organisations – yet if you could use a system to help people with their thinking to enable them to identify different, quicker, more effective actions leading to greater results, wouldn't that actually save you and your organisation a great deal of time and money?

Who is this book for?

This book is for Managers who are serious about business improvement, irrespective of size of organisation or seniority. It's as straightforward as that.

An offer

Jo and I know from our experience of using this material on the leadership and business improvement programmes we run that this book will give you plenty to think about and a lot of ideas about what you could do next.

So here's an offer for you. When you have finished reading, request your free 20-minute organisational change telephone coaching session with a Go MAD Thinking Engineer, by emailing your contact details to change@gomadthinking.com.

One of our team will help you with your thinking and you'll leave the conversation with a clearly defined goal and plan of action about what to do next.

"If the rate of change on the outside exceeds the rate of change on the inside, the end is near."
Jack Welch

Making the case for different thinking during change

You may just be reading this page to decide whether it will be worthwhile you spending the time to read this book. You may be thinking that managing the people side of change is about soft and fluffy text book stuff and has no place in an operational results and task focused environment. So before I start, let's make the business case for doing something different about the way you plan, implement and act during organisational change.

First, list all the changes that are currently happening in your organisation. These changes could be process changes, relocation, restructuring, implementation of new systems or policies, people leaving or joining the team, mergers, budget cuts or new initiatives. They can be big or small changes. You'll probably find there are quite a few happening at the same time!

Changes happening in my organisation:

A quick calculation

Calculate your answers to the following questions:

a)   How many employees are likely to be affected by the changes you
     have listed in your organisation?

                         _____ employees

b)   On average how much non-productive time is spent per week by
     each employee reacting against the changes or on worrying,
     gossiping, speculating and rumour mongering activities?

                         _____ hours

c)   How many weeks has this been going on for?

                         _____ weeks

d)   How many weeks will it continue to go on for if left unchecked?

                         _____ weeks

Calculation 1: a x b x c =

This is the number of lost hours in your organisation so far.

Calculation 2: a x b x d =

This is the number of additional hours that could potentially be lost.

Calculation 3: (calculation 1 + calculation 2) x the average employee
hourly rate =

This is how much it could be costing you in monetary terms.

Calculation 3 doesn't include, for example, the missed opportunity for higher profit or exceptional customer service during this period. So in reality this cost is probably much higher.

Now you have the business case, how motivated are you to make a difference about managing change?

Just think of the impact you could make if your people could possibly be helped to adapt and accept change in 3 months instead of 6 months.

So, this book is not about planning, organising or managing change. It is about practical tips, tools and techniques that will have a positive impact on people and help them to more easily and quickly accept change; it is about you helping them to increase their productivity and effectiveness within the organisation. This is about business improvement.

"Commitment is the enemy of resistance, for it is the serious promise to press on, to get up, no matter how many times you are knocked down."
David McNally

Reading alone cannot develop your skills or motivation. I am aware of this limitation and so encourage you to apply the words you read to real situations and real individuals whom it is possible to help. So make notes, complete the exercises (go back and do the calculation if you have skipped that bit), highlight sections you want to refer back to and write thoughts alongside the text.

There are notes pages at the back of the book to capture your thoughts and the actions you might want to take after reading this book. Challenge yourself to get to a minimum of 20 by the time you have finished reading.

Many managers believe that knowing what to do in times of change is sufficient. This is not enough on its own. A committed positive intention to make a difference is also needed.

If you are serious about making a difference for yourself, your team and your organisation, then proceed to the next page and get ready to increase your probability of success during organisational change.

"Knowing is not enough; we must apply.
Willing is not enough; we must do."
Johann Wolfgang von Goethe

PART ONE: ESSENTIAL INFORMATION

1. The "Secret"

There is a little-known secret to managing organisational change effectively. When you discover it, in these next few pages, and understand the underlying principles you will no doubt reflect that much of it is common sense. However common sense and common practice are very different. I should know, having worked since 1991 with thousands of managers in hundreds of organisations. Much of this work has involved helping middle and senior managers increase their effectiveness during restructuring, downsizing, mergers, management buy-outs and various forms of cultural change.

Change vs Transition

Before "the secret" is revealed, let's make sure that we have a common understanding of a few terms and phrases.

The first is "change" or more precisely that which is referred to as change within your organisation. I have found that when change is mentioned, it usually means "things" changing, for example, systems, procedures, ways of working, location, behaviour, company ownership, etc. Usually you are able to see the change or even touch the results of it. Hence, change is something that is external to your body.

Think about the changes in your organisation that you listed earlier. You will probably have noticed that individuals react in different ways and at different speeds. There are many reasons why this happens:

- Some people are more adaptable to change than others.
- Some people resist change more than others.
- Some people have more to lose than others.
- Some people have developed stronger habits than others.
- Some people deny change is happening or will happen.

- Some people don't realise the full extent of the change.
- Some people feel exposed by change.

Whatever the reasons, the fact is individuals, including you, react internally to the external change. Before you, or anyone in your organisation fully accepts any change, an internal process of adjustment has to happen. This internal process is called "transition".

There are two important things to note here. Firstly, that change (external process) is different from transition (internal process). Secondly, changes to things in the workplace happen at a different speed to people's acceptance of the change (the transition process). A practical example of this is when a change in working hours or shift patterns is introduced. The change happens overnight, whereas the transition can take considerably longer. I have worked in many companies where it has taken several years for employees to accept such changes.

"All the great leaders have had one characteristic in common: it was the willingness to confront unequivocally the major anxiety of their people in their time. This, and not much else, is the essence of leadership."
John Kenneth Galbraith

TIME TO THINK

I invite you to stop reading for a moment and think of an example in your organisation of a past change that has been implemented where people did not immediately accept it. (I will ask you to refer back to your example later, so make sure you have chosen one!)

My example of organisational change:

Now let's move on to "the secret" of managing change effectively. The reason that change is often unsuccessful is related to management's perception of change and how to manage it. Many managers I encounter consider the planning, logistics, systems, procedures and the physical factors that need changing. Very few, even at the most senior level, place much emphasis on the people issues, particularly their likely reaction to change.

How many times have you attended meetings about implementing change, when the outcomes have been task-focused actions involving feasibility, logistics and planning? Managers who are good at planning and logistics often do not make the time, or have the inclination to spend time, considering the people issues.

Consider your own organisation: are the people transition issues built into your master schedule or project plan? I have been called into companies on numerous occasions where a major organisational change has been implemented with detailed precision according to plan, yet caused a massive negative reaction in the workforce. Much of this reaction could have been easily foreseen and overcome if the managers had only been aware of "the secret".

The secret is simple – in order for change to be effective, transition must happen.

In other words, unless individuals are helped to adapt and accept the change, the change will not have the desired impact on the business.

In your calculation you have already established that you can save your organisation potentially tens of thousands of hours and hundreds of thousands of pounds by successfully managing people through the transition. In fact several years ago one of my clients calculated that as a result of ignoring people's reactions to a merger twelve months earlier, the company had wasted approximately 300,000 hours of time or the equivalent of over £3 million. When asked how he had arrived at these figures, he gave the following reasoning:

"We have 3,000 employees who on average have spent approximately two hours per week during the past year engaging in non-productive activities and working against the changes we have implemented. 300,000 hours at £12 per hour is £3.6 million. What's more, until managers help their people to accept change (transition) these figures will continue."

There are three further pieces of information additional to "the secret" that you need to know if you want to save your organisation valuable time and money. I have shared this information with thousands of managers and refined it to the following areas:

1. People's reaction to organisational change – the four underlying causes of a negative reaction to change.
2. Adapting to and accepting change – the three-stage process of most use to managers.
3. Organisational factors which can help or hinder change – the five factors with the greatest impact on the morale of people.

So, let's explain each of these in turn and illustrate them with some practical examples.

2. The Four Underlying Causes Of A Negative Reaction To Change

Over the years I have worked closely with Jo Stead, who is one of the leading UK researchers into the negative reactions experienced by individuals in response to organisational change. I have simplified her findings into the following underlying causes:

1. **A sense of unfairness in the way that employees have been treated.** This is most commonly based upon unwritten beliefs and assumptions formed over a period of time that the way things were done around here would always continue. This has been termed the "psychological contract" between employer and employee. Hence, when change is introduced by the organisation it is deemed unfair by the individual.

Managers often know that it will be seen as unfair by the employees and make comments such as, "I know they will be unhappy about this...". Yet it is interesting to note that while many managers know this very few take action to address these thoughts.

If this underlying cause exists in your organisation, you might hear comments such as, "It's not fair"; "We have never had to do it this way before" and, "After everything that I/we have done, look what they have decided…".

2. **Personal uncertainty and insecurity about the future.** It is usual to find that most individuals spend time thinking about the impact of organisational change upon themselves, their current role and possible future prospects. This happens even when people are not directly affected by the change. I have come across several cases when key people, including senior managers, have become unduly convinced that they are likely to lose their jobs. This can lead to people doing a variety of things in an attempt to protect their current position, resulting in stress.

    If this underlying cause exists in your organisation, you might notice an unwillingness to make decisions, an increase in defensive behaviour, and increased speculation and rumour.

3. **Perceived powerlessness.** The larger the organisation, the greater the tendency is for individuals to feel that changes are imposed upon them. Common phrases that might be heard include, "There is nothing that we can do"; "They don't ask us for our opinions"; "It's them and us. They tell us and we just have to accept it" and, "Head Office have decided…".

    I have found that most people want to be involved, even in some small way, in change and their natural tendency is to seek to participate by giving suggestions and being heard. When this is perceived as futile, or changes are made outside their sphere of influence, their feelings of powerlessness may result in a lack of commitment or real interest. Examples of this are commonly seen in many organisations when new corporate logos, mission statements and competencies are introduced without consultation with the workforce.

4. **Resisting the need to adapt to change.** When things change in the workplace a need is created for individuals to adapt. If individuals do not accept the change by making the necessary transition, their external behaviour and performance will not be as effective as it could be.

    This internal resistance will vary tremendously between individuals. With some, the resistance is minimal or non-existent and with others, it will last for ten years or even longer. Common phrases to listen out for include, "I don't see the point"; "I'm just going to carry on"; "This change is a mistake"; "It's just the latest management fad" and, "It won't work, it's a waste of time".

A Common Theme: Self-Talk

All of the four causes have something in common – the way in which people will be talking inwardly to themselves and outwardly to each other.

If you look at the example phrases I gave in each of those four causes they were all examples of what I call "hindering thoughts" – the opposite of which is "helpful thoughts". On average we talk to ourselves every 11 seconds. So during change it is quite reasonable to assume that the words and phrases you hear, as a reaction to change, from your team are just the tip of the iceberg in terms of the quantity and nature of thoughts they may be having about the change. Notice your self-talk too – is it helpful or hindering?

Hindering thoughts are those that get in the way of moving forward towards a solution or goal, or in this case the acceptance of a change. Helpful thoughts will help you move forward towards acceptance and create sustained results. It is perfectly normal to have hindering thoughts – the key to handling this as a manager is to recognise both your own hindering thoughts and those of others, and to choose to do something about them.

TIME TO THINK

Remind yourself of the example you selected earlier of when people did not immediately accept the change. Consider the underlying reasons for their reaction. Write down the words and phrases you heard people using under each of the four causes. Also add in any other behaviours that you noticed that may indicate one of the underlying reasons for a negative reaction to change.

A sense of unfairness	Personal uncertainty and insecurity
Perceived powerlessness	Resisting the need to adapt to change

Q: Think about who was saying/doing what – what did you notice about the variety of individual reactions to change?

Q: What if you were to add in your own reactions at the time – your words and behaviours? What could you learn about your own reactions to organisational change?

I am sure that you can identify these four underlying causes in other examples of organisational change you have experienced. Maybe you can even recognise the causes of some of your own reactions in the past. It is okay to admit to having them. In fact it will probably be useful to remember those examples when we move on to helping others adapt to change. Later, I will reveal the three key management tasks that will help you to address the underlying causes of negative reaction to change I have just outlined. However, before focusing on what you can do, I invite you to continue developing your knowledge and understanding of transition.

"When written in Chinese, the word crisis is composed of two characters. One represents danger, and the other represents opportunity."
John F. Kennedy

3. Adapting To Change – A Three-Stage Process

"I wish people would just accept things." How many times have you heard a similar phrase or sentiment? I know that I have certainly used it in the past! It would be really handy if people would immediately accept change and continue working at high levels of performance as if nothing had happened. But that is fantasy.

This is extremely unlikely to happen. Yet, many organisations continue to make major changes and act as if they expect it to happen. Why does it continue? Because senior and middle managers are largely unaware of the process that individuals go through in adapting to change. Plus they have had longer themselves to understand and adapt and of course they have focused virtually all their efforts on the logistics and planning of change.

The process about to be explained is based on a very simple three-stage model by William Bridges of how individuals adapt to change.

ENDINGS ⟶ TRANSITION ⟶ BEGINNINGS

Endings: When a change happens, some things end – often forever. All change involves loss and this naturally upsets some people more than others. Imagine a large-scale organisational change or company restructuring. This might result in several of the following endings:

- Role and responsibilities (including favourite tasks).
- Contact with the people you work with.
- Personal status.
- Work environment.
- Familiar ways of doing things.
- Beliefs about what it means to work in this organisation.
- Expectations about your future career.

Before we expect others to accept the change it is vital that we understand that they have to let go and end certain things. The process of letting go does not happen instantly. Often initial feelings of shock and denial about the change are replaced by more intense feelings of anger or sadness, as there is a gradual realisation of the full implications of the change.

The line-manager has a key role to play in helping people to deal with these endings. Unfortunately many managers are either unaware of this or do not possess the necessary skills (outlined later in Part Two). For the time being it is important to recognise that it is natural for individuals to feel this way in response to change.

The transition stage: After endings have been made, an individual's attitude towards the change is likely to be more negative than before the change took place. Once the implications of the change have been fully realised, there begins a phase of exploration and discovery.

Think of a time when you had to learn about new systems or understand revised expectations. Can you remember the experience of gradually adapting, whilst also feeling frustrated and confused at times? This transition stage involves learning, very often in the absence of role models. Let's give an example.

Go MAD Thinking were helping with the restructuring of a large manufacturing company. This involved, among many things, centralising the stock control system of three factories on the same site. A new computer system was introduced integrating the purchasing with stock control. Many people reacted against the change mainly because much of what they were familiar with had ended. Even after dealing with the endings they still experienced great frustration with the new system as they struggled to learn and adapt to new ways of working. The management had no greater technical expertise than their people and so were unable to resolve much of the confusion. By helping people with their thinking we ensured, over a period of time, that the system was run efficiently and everyone began to see and appreciate its benefit.

You might be wondering what the significance of this example is. Well, there are a number of key learning points:

- People felt negative about the change before feeling better.
- The transition stage cannot be skipped or ignored. It has to be worked through. The transition stage does not fit a neatly defined timescale.
- The managers, although unable to help technically, made a tremendous difference in helping their people adapt to change. They did this by understanding the transition process and applying relevant skills and techniques to ensure it progressed. The change (i.e. the system) was effected relatively quickly and smoothly.
- The reactions to change were predictable and managers were trained in advance to handle the people issues that result from change.

Beginnings: If in change some things will end, then it follows that there will be things that begin. Acknowledgement of those new things is as important as the acknowledgement of endings. When the change becomes considered as normal practice then you will know that the beginnings stage has begun.

4. The Transition Curve

You will find the following graph useful in understanding further how individuals react to organisational change. This is adapted from several different models and I have used it to help many managers over recent years.

THE TRANSITION CURVE

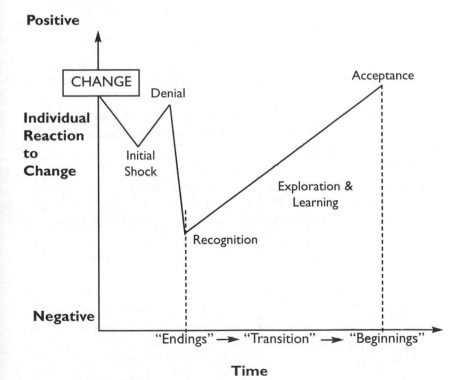

Whilst this is a generalised model, in that it does not apply to everyone all of the time, in every change situation, it is useful to understand the following points:

- The old has to end, before the new is accepted.
- Individuals will react negatively before acceptance is reached.
- Some individuals remain in denial for longer than others.
- The strongest emotions are usually on the steepest part of the graph i.e. as individuals begin to, and then fully recognise, the implications of the change.
- Exploration is a more gradual process which takes time.
- The timescale for individuals to go through the stages will differ.
- It is pointless to expect people to accept change without them first going through the transition process.

The Marathon Effect

It can be useful here to use the analogy of a marathon race to describe what happens in teams and organisations during change and transition.

Let's take the London Marathon for example. In that event there are thousands of people taking part. There will be many different 'variables' going on for individuals:

- Motivation for wanting to complete the event will vary – to raise money, to be the best in the world, to beat last year's time, as a competition to beat others, to have fun, to prove to themselves they can do it. For some it is a race – for others it is a fun day out.
- Self-belief – some will know without any doubt that they can achieve it and others may harbour thoughts that they won't complete the course. Some will have helpful memories they can rely on from when they ran a marathon before, others will be recalling hindering memories of not finishing events at school and talking themselves out of success.

- Planning and preparation – some will have trained for years possibly with a bigger goal in mind – such as the Olympics. Others will see completion of this event as the most amazing achievement in their life. The longer-term goal may be different.
- Outfits – some will be dressed in the running clothes and shoes made from the latest "go fast" technology, others may be wearing a giant costume of a cartoon character. The first strides through the course with ease, the second has to take smaller steps, finds it clumsy and awkward and maybe has to take a breather along the way.
- The finish line and the length of the course are in the same place for everybody, yet there can be hours, and sometimes days, between the time of the fastest finisher and the time of the slowest finisher. Some, choose to not finish the course.

The journey of transition is very like a marathon. People will have different reasons for wanting to get through the change, some will feel like giving up and potentially some won't make it through to acceptance. The perspective from the front, if you are leading change, is very different compared to being at the "tail end" of change as you will be in different places on the transition curve.

As the leader of a change you may have spent months planning and preparing the change, you may feel completely prepared, confident and motivated and wanting to see the results of your change with immediate effect. When the change is announced and others hear about it for the first time (i.e. cross the start line), the senior team who are way ahead (i.e. the pace setters) are very much focused on the end (i.e. the finishing line).

So it may come as a surprise that you don't have a team of "elite runners" behind you. Think about the person in the hippopotamus costume. People are not likely to move through transition in an orderly group, at the same speed, in the same direction and without further support. These runners may feel poorly equipped and their goal and motivations in this change may not be the same as yours. They may not have the right equipment and every day they may be talking to themselves and others about how the change is hard, difficult and a waste of time, or how they tried it before and it didn't work.

"Expect resistance - and take it as feedback....it is said that if you don't get any resistance to change you are in danger of missing some vital flaw in your plan!"
Jenny Briggs

TIME TO THINK

Now think back once more to your example of a previous change. Pick a point in time shortly after the change was announced. Focus on the reactions of people in your organisation. Remember their behaviour, actions and what they said. It is useful to locate where people were on the transition curve – you will then be able to see the stages people were at in their transition journey. Use the following table to review where you think people were. Start with yourself.

Who	Where on the curve?	How I know this: words and behaviours

5. The Five Organisational Factors Which Are Most Likely To Help Or Hinder People During Change

Much of the information and knowledge shared with you so far relates to the process of transition that starts inside a person's mind and then shows through their behaviour. Before moving on to how this information can be practically applied, let's briefly explain the five major organisational factors which influence an individual's reaction to change.

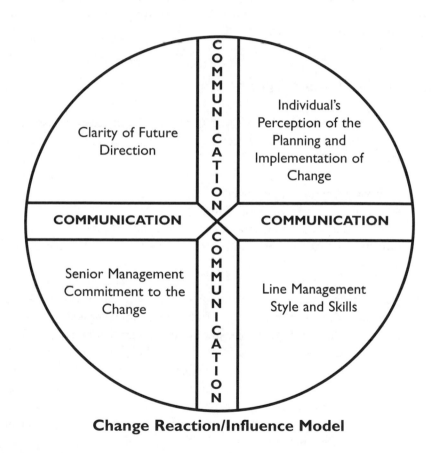

Change Reaction/Influence Model

1. Communication

Imagine for a moment, that the diagram on the previous page is a gigantic hot cross bun, as large as it could possibly be, and you are standing in the middle of it. As you look around you can see and are affected by activities in each of the four quadrants. All around you, information is whizzing by as you stand in the centre of the communication crossroads. You notice that the more helpful information about change appears to come from certain quadrants, whereas rumour, speculation and mixed messages tend to come from other quadrants.

2. Clarity of future direction

When change happens in organisations, research has shown the importance of having a future direction that is clearly communicated and enables the workforce to:

-   be involved in moving forward
-   feel inspired by the vision and mission
-   receive positive, optimistic and consistent messages
-   understand that the best aspects of the past are still being retained.

This last point is important to remember, as all too often I experience organisations who sell the benefits of change by focusing solely on the future. In their vain attempts to get people to accept change quickly, they often completely overlook the fact that individuals need to make endings first. This can create greater insecurity and uncertainty in the minds of individuals who are not yet ready to accept the messages. Instead, be more effective by balancing the benefits of change with deliberate reassurance about familiar ways and practices that will continue to happen in the future.

"Don't be afraid to tweak your plan or change some of your tools – it shows you're listening to feedback and making sure you get the right desired end result."
Nicola Stout

3. Senior management commitment to the change

The Senior Management team need to be seen as strong, inspirational and unified in acting in accordance with the mission and goals. At times of major change, their commitment will be examined in detail by people to spot any inconsistencies and weaknesses. Failure to act as role models and change champions will undoubtedly affect the morale of others and the speed at which change is implemented.

"Have compelling sponsorship – ensure there is proactive sponsorship for the change from senior management. Without this it is very unlikely the change will meet the intended results."
Michael Gould

4. Perception of the planning and implementation of change

Whilst individuals are obviously affected by the planning and implementation of change, their perception of its effectiveness is likely to differ widely from those involved in the planning. I have worked with several organisations where the planning was meticulous, detailed and well thought through. Yet because it was done by a small group of people perceived as remote and inaccessible, people were unaware of how good the plan was. In fact the only thing that these organisations hadn't planned for was how to manage the people reaction!

Remember "the secret" – in order for change to be effective, transition must happen.

"Have the courage to cry out 'the emperor has no clothes' if you think the proposed change is ill conceived or thought through – and then help the emperor get dressed!"
Simon Wilson

5. Line management style and skills

The fourth quadrant relates to the style and skills of line-managers in managing change and specifically to their interaction with people. Arguably, this is the most influential factor as the day-to-day actions of a line-manager will either help or hinder people with the process of transition. The following section focuses on many of the key skills and will enable you to assess your own ability and those of other managers in your organisation.

One final thought before leaving the "hot cross bun" diagram. It is possible to use this model when planning and reviewing change to identify:

- Where is communication likely to be more and less effective?
- Which quadrant is most likely to help or hinder effective change?
- Which areas of organisational weakness need to be addressed?

TIME TO THINK

Using your example of organisational change answer the questions below to diagnose which areas of the "hot cross bun" could have benefited from more attention.

1. Communication: When the changes were communicated...	Yes	No
Information concerning decisions taken was openly available to employees		
There was a good flow of information from top down		
There were good opportunities for feeding back opinions and queries		
Individuals were clearly informed how they personally would be affected		
New objectives and expectations were clearly explained		

2. Clarity of future direction: When looking to the future of the organisation...	Yes	No
The future appeared bright		
There was a clear vision and goals		
Real efforts were made to encourage ownership of the vision and goals		
The best aspects of the past were being retained		
The employees were valued by the organisation		

3.	Senior management commitment: during the changes, senior management...	Yes	No
	Were out and about championing the changes		
	Were visibly committed to the future of the organisation		
	Clearly supported the decisions taken		
	Shared a common view of where the organisation was heading		
	Considered the effect of their actions on employees		

4.	Perception of the planning: When the changes were planned...	Yes	No
	Care was taken to treat people fairly		
	There was wide involvement in the planning process		
	There were well publicised timescales for implementation		
	The rationale for decisions was made clear to employees		
	Practical implications of decisions were carefully thought through		

5. Line management style and skills: During the changes, in general, line management...	Yes	No
Actively promoted the changes at the local level		
Passed on information openly to their staff		
Encouraged involvement in the implementation of changes		
Were concerned and supportive towards individuals in their team		
Were sensitive in their treatment of those losing out in the changes		

"In theory, practice and theory are the same.
In practice they are not."
Albert Einstein

PART TWO:
ESSENTIAL SKILLS TO MOVE FORWARD

Having read the previous pages, you now have the necessary background information to make a difference. Based on experience you are probably in the top 1% of managers in terms of knowledge about change and the reactions it causes. Now let's move on to consider effective ways of applying this knowledge.

By now you'll have recognised that the process of individual transition cannot be avoided. It can be speeded up and this is a key role for line-managers during organisational change. **If you can help your team to move more quickly through the endings and transition stages to acceptance, you will reap the benefits of the change through increased individual productivity and improved team performance.** To ensure this happens, your actions need to address the four underlying causes of a negative reaction to change.

At this stage there is good news and there is bad news to share with you. The bad news is that one of the four underlying causes cannot be resolved in the short-term. This is the perceived breaking of the psychological contract – the sense of unfairness in the way that employees have been treated. This break in the psychological contract cannot be repaired quickly, as it requires line and senior managers to consistently act fairly over a longer time frame. Even then, trust may be difficult to restore.

The good news is that the remaining three underlying causes can be addressed by your day-to-day line-management actions. There are three key tasks, which Go MAD Thinking Engineer, Kathryn Roberts concisely describes as "The Three I's".

1. Information and explanation
2. Involvement
3. Individual attention

6. The Three I's

1. Information and explanation

Personal uncertainty and insecurity about the future naturally causes individuals to seek further information and have questions answered. If the uncertainty and insecurity still remains, then this results in the desire for even more information and so on. There is probably not an organisation experiencing change, where everyone is totally satisfied with the amount or type of information they receive.

> *"Tell people everything; nothing is too small to bother them with. Let the people filter out what is not for them rather than assuming what people do and do not need to know."*
> *Judith Marples*

A useful starting point is to help individuals understand and accept the need to change. To do this the following five questions need to be answered either on a one-to-one basis or as a group, for example in a team meeting.

- What specific events brought about the changes in our organisation?
- Why was there a need to change?
- Who was involved in the decision making process?
- What other options were considered and why were they rejected?
- What is the change intended to achieve?

Before you do this be sure that you have given some thought to your answers and checked them out for consistency with other managers. This might sound obvious but you would be surprised at the wide variation in answers given by managers in the same organisation. So, take nothing for granted.

Even if people are not asking these questions for you to hear, the chances are that they are asking themselves or each other. You might even have asked them yourself. Often during change, information intended to assist people can have the opposite affect when communicated poorly. The following notice-board bulletin was brought to my attention. The names have been changed to protect the innocent, but otherwise it is reproduced exactly.

Attention
Team Change

As from today, Tom Jenkins has replaced Steve Howarth as Quality Assurance Manager and will now report directly to Peter Mackintosh. 9th December.

If you worked in this recently merged organisation, particularly if you knew Steve Howarth, what thoughts might go through your mind? Probably very similar questions to those previously mentioned.

- What has caused this change?
- Why has Tom replaced Steve?
- Who made the decision?
- What is happening to Steve?
- What difference will it make?

It might cause you to question the planning and implementation of change, as so little information is included and the short notice given. For most, if not all, of the 480 employees it raised more questions and created greater uncertainty then intended. I certainly witnessed a large amount of talk and speculation about the notice for the next four days. Now, let us estimate the possible time and cost implications of this example.

If each of the 480 employees was negatively affected by this notice (speculating, gossiping or worrying to themselves) for 30 minutes, it totals 240 hours. This is the equivalent of one person working for six weeks or in financial terms one and a half months salary. All caused by a memo that probably took less than two minutes to write! If only the writer had spent ten minutes and answered the five key questions, a considerable amount of time, worth several thousand pounds, could have been saved.

I mentioned this to the Human Resources Director who admitted responsibility and asked for help. In less than 15 minutes he had gained the answers to the five questions and had written the following alternative.

UPDATE INFORMATION ON QUALITY SYSTEMS
from Peter Mackintosh
(Divisional Director)

Following the merger with Engineer Co. plc, there has been a need to standardise our quality procedures to ensure consistency, both internally and to our customers.

Over the past 3 weeks, Steve Howarth and Tom Jenkins have led a review of both existing quality systems and involved the 12 department heads from both sites. 17 of the 22 procedures have been identified as closely compatible and require little or no modification. The remaining 5 procedures relate mainly to document transfer and storage, where both sites have previously identified that improvements needed to be made.

Rather than adopt either of the existing site procedures, I have decided to invest time and resource in ensuring we have an effective and efficient way of handling this critical area of our business. Steve Howarth, in his new role of Systems Manager, will continue to provide assistance to Tom Jenkins who will manage this project for the next 3 months and report direct to myself. Please give Tom your full assistance.

Thank you

The skill in writing information about change is to consider it from the reader's viewpoint:

- What will their reaction be? Will they have helpful or hindering thoughts?
- What questions will it cause them to ask?
- What further information will they require?
- How can you demonstrate that the change has been planned and implemented effectively?

"Communicate in down to earth language at least weekly – even if there is nothing to tell."
Steve Ogle

TIME TO THINK

Now consider the example of change in your organisation by answering the following questions:

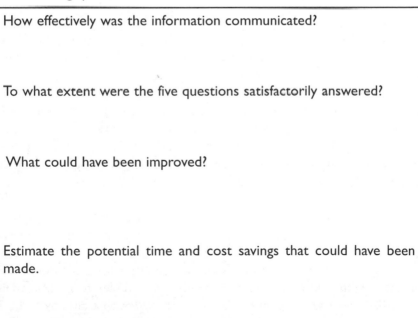

How effectively was the information communicated?

To what extent were the five questions satisfactorily answered?

What could have been improved?

Estimate the potential time and cost savings that could have been made.

"What do I communicate about the change when there is no new information available?"

This is a common question asked by managers, usually in the context of restructuring, buy-outs, mergers and acquisitions, but could equally apply to any change that has long been talked about. Often managers feel it is best not to say anything if there is no new information and the situation is still unclear. This does nothing to help the individual who is feeling insecure and uncertain about the future.

It is more helpful if you can firstly acknowledge that some things are still unclear. Secondly, give a specific date or milestone by when you expect more information to be available. If you say more information will be available in June, your people will expect something from the 1st June, and the gossiping and rumours will start up again as June progresses without any communication! So my tip would be to go for 1st July to build yourself a cushion of time, with the intent of communicating something at some point in June.

There is always a reason why information is currently unavailable. For example, a decision needs to be made at next month's meeting or certain processes and procedures might need to be carried out before further information is available.

It is still possible to give explanations about the process which will eventually lead to questions being answered. Whilst this does not remove the uncertainty, for many it provides some relief in knowing that their manager is in a similar position to themselves, has no further information, but is aware of key dates and milestones.

There will be a need to repeat information and explanations several times. An individual might be in the denial stage of the transition curve and perhaps acting as if the change is not happening. If this is the case, you might need to repeat the same information several times using different communication methods before it is understood. Hopefully you will never use the excuse, "But I've told them that already". I have seen examples of people being given the same information about change at least six or seven times with no apparent reaction or acknowledgement. Yet the next time the information is given they treat it as if they have just received it for the first time!

2. Involvement

Obviously, individuals cannot be involved in every aspect relating to change. However, if there is a total lack of involvement in the change then the perception of being powerless will increase. As a skilful manager, it is always possible to involve people in some aspect of the change, however small that might be.

One of the easiest ways of ensuring people's involvement during change is to have participative meetings on a regular basis.

> **TIME TO THINK**

Examine the way you conduct meetings and consider how involved others are:

How many of the agenda items are suggested by your team?

To what extent do you allow them to contribute during meetings?

How much encouragement and responsibility do you give individuals to take actions and develop ideas following a meeting?

What could you possibly do differently to get them involved?

"Read the body language in the room constantly – bodies don't lie and you will know support and resistance instantly."
Beth Chadwick

The Go MAD® Thinking System

Using a thinking system as a way of involving others is a great way to give people a common language and toolkit. The Go MAD® Thinking System, based on 4000 hours of research, is a framework for natural success. Comprised of seven principles with 11 link lines, it enables you to take a solution focused approach to your thinking that is both straightforward and practical. Because it is a system it is important to pay attention to all principles and the inter-connections between them. By doing this you will create a set of actions that will lead you to the results you desire, more creatively, consistently, quickly and efficiently.

If you want to understand more about the Go MAD® Thinking System, and how it can be universally applied to any situation, I recommend you read, "Go MAD – The Art of Making a Difference".

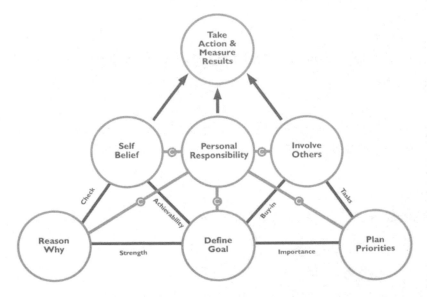

The Go MAD® Framework

Here, I have combined its application in change management with its excellent use as a coaching tool to create a set of questions based around the seven principles. These questions, which can be used in a group session, will help people to think and get them involved.

Reason Why	What are the reasons for the current change?
	What are the implications of doing nothing?
	What else do we need to understand about the reasons for change?
	What is the most compelling reason for change?
Define Goal	What is the objective?
	What are we working towards?
	What do we want to achieve? (Note: the goal might be an existing operational objective or relate to resolving a current problem or concern.)
Self-Belief	How confident are you feeling that we can move forward on a scale of 1 to 10?
	What is the level of self-belief that we can achieve the goal?
	What can we do to develop or maintain our level of self-belief?
Plan	What are the known options?
	What are the possible tasks and resources that could help us?
	What possible things could get in the way and how could we overcome them?
	Which options are highest priority?
	How much time do we need to set aside?

Involve Others	Who else is involved?
	What possible reasons might there be to involve others?
	Who else could we possibly involve?
	How will we involve them and obtain their commitment?
Personal Responsibility	What will we do and by when?
	Who will do what?
	How committed are we?
Take Action & Measure Results	When will we review our progress?

"In times of change, organisations, quite rightly, want to move quickly and this can result in pressure to 'do stuff'. Encourage the sponsor to make sure they are really clear about what they are trying to achieve, and why, and to consider a broad range of possibilities and implications before jumping to implementation. The most constructive way of doing this without appearing as a brake or blocker is to use some really good questions to develop the thinking."
Simon Wilson

Here are some additional suggestions for increasing the levels of involvement:

Identify endings as a team and discuss the implications of each ending. You could use several of the example endings mentioned earlier to prompt their thoughts. Be attentive to how individuals react during this discussion, as some are likely to become more aware than others of what will be lost.

You might need to follow up the meeting with one-to-one discussions to help some individuals manage their endings. I recognise that you might not feel comfortable with this task. Many managers avoid doing it and hence some of their people never fully let go of the past. In the long-term this avoidance costs time and money. If you feel that you want to build your confidence in helping your teams manage endings, make a note now of what action you could take, what resources might be useful and who could help you so that you feel comfortable with this key skill in the future.

Identify, as a team, what will stay the same as a result of the change. This can be anything however big or small and can help people to realise that not everything is changing.

Help individuals to identify those factors that are the "givens" of a situation (i.e. pre-determined decisions about the change which are outside their control and hence cannot be influenced) and differentiate them from the things that are in their control and/or can be influenced.

Do some possibility thinking around ways of moving forward and overcoming obstacles. When possibility thinking give yourself and the team the rule "anything goes" and give people permission to be as creative as they like, reassuring them that there will be opportunity to evaluate the possibilities afterwards. Ensure that any possibilities you offer are not given undue emphasis or weight due to your position in the team. Hold back on any judgements or evaluating while the team explores possibilities.

Delegate responsibility for exploring and investigating alternative ways of doing things in the future. This will help to reduce the sense of powerless and lack of control.

Encourage people to report back their findings and seek the opinions of the rest of the team. This will ensure everyone stays involved and feeling that they are receiving regular communication updates.

Ask their opinion about an aspect of the change that is affecting them. This is probably the most simple and quickest way to increase an individual's involvement. It only takes a couple of minutes, yet can make a massive difference to someone feeling powerless.

"Never tell people how to do things. Tell them what to do and they will surprise you with their ingenuity."
George Patton

3. Individual attention

If you manage more than one person, you will have recognised that individuals react to change differently. You will also now be more aware of why this happens. In order to fully understand the reasons why people resist the need to adapt to change you have to give individual attention to each person. People worry about different things for different reasons and will take a different amount of time to move through the transition curve and accept change.

A key skill is to identify who in your team is most affected by the change. Whilst past behaviour is usually a good indicator of future behaviour, a different change will mean different endings and hence possibly a different reaction. A starting point is to consider what will end for each person as a result of the change. Also consider from their perspective what they feel might be lost in the future. For some people these endings will be welcomed and seen as opportunities, but for many others, they will result in things being missed.

A few years ago I worked with Michael, a Divisional Director in a large UK service organisation undergoing massive restructuring. His role remained largely unaffected and his work continued much as before. However, he was deeply affected by the change because something important for him had ended. His career goal was no longer applicable. For the past six years Michael had set his sights on a certain position on the main board of directors. That position had now disappeared. Fortunately, his manager realised this ending and the importance of giving individual attention. In many other organisations, this would have gone unnoticed and the individual would have taken much longer to make the transition.

"Don't be deceived – you must not think that you will save a huge amount of your time and effort by setting up briefing sessions or communication processes because your people will still need your attention – disregard them at your peril. Remember that people take time."
Keith Sparrow

It may not be appropriate to manage endings in a group meeting, particularly if you have already identified that some individuals within the team will experience substantially more or greater losses than others. This is when it is important to talk with people on an individual basis. I have identified 10 key points to bear in mind when doing this.

1. Clearly explain the reason for the meeting. Notice the difference between saying, "Can I see you in my office?" (possibly intimidating and causing fear of reprisal) and, "I would like to have a chat with you about the recent changes to see what I can do to help you".

2. It can be useful to mention in advance that you intend to have short meetings with each person. Again, be careful about clearly explaining the purpose of these meetings.

3. Plan in advance of the meeting. What issues and concerns might you anticipate?

4. Notice how each individual reacts when you meet with them. Their body language, tone of voice and eye contact will all give you clues about what is happening inside the person and how they are reacting to the change.

5. Use questions such as, "What are your thoughts about the change?" or, "What's going through your mind right now?" The answers to these questions will give you clues as to whether their thoughts are helpful or hindering, and how you may be able to help them.

6. Avoid selling the future and the benefits of change. Focus on their concerns, not your agenda.

7. Listen with the aim of understanding rather than listening with the aim of being able to spot when you can interrupt to get your point across!

8. Agree any actions for either you or them.

9. Agree a follow-up review. This will help the individual to feel that you are committed to helping them on more than a one-off occasion.

10. As you listen, identify where they might be on the transition curve. Listed below are approaches and strategies that you will find helpful in encouraging individuals to move towards the next stage.

Initial Shock	Encourage them to talk about their understanding of the change and the information they have received about it.
	Clarify what has been understood.
	Identify and provide any missing information.
	If necessary, give them space to think things through.

Denial	Provide information.
	Repeat information in different ways.
	Talk about changes and implications (endings).
	Confront them (non-aggressively) with reality and the need for change.
	Encourage them to ask questions.
	Bring them into contact with others who have moved forward.

Recognition	Let them have their say and express feelings.
	Acknowledge their feelings without accepting blame.
	Re-emphasise and explain the reasons for change.
	Help them to identify and manage endings.
	Start to promote positives (without being too pushy).
	Allow them time, but ensure the work continues.

Exploration	Reassure that others are unsure and unclear about certain things.
	Establish what is unclear and clarify.
	Be patient with requests for information and possible confusion.
	Find ways of involving them and allowing a sense of control over some aspect of work.

Acceptance	Don't stop. Keep on using the three I's – Information and explanation, Involvement and Individual attention.

Look back at the exercise you did where you located people on the Transition Curve based on their actions and behaviour. Consider how you might use the above strategies with your team.

> *"Listen to your people; they will spot things going wrong long before you would."*
> *Ben Reid*

The 10 minute challenge

I was challenged by Brian, an experienced manufacturing manager, about the emphasis I was placing on the people issues. His point was that he had a factory to run, equipment to commission and operating changes to make. He talked at length about all the tangible hard aspects of change – planning, feasibility studies, actions, timescales, and implementation reports – without once mentioning the people, except to say they had low morale. He wanted to know what he could do to improve their morale without spending much time doing it! I established that Brian had eight people directly reporting to him, and a further 90 people below them. I asked him if he could spare each of his direct reports just 10 minutes of his time this month? He stated he could easily do this, but asked what he should do with this 10 minute slot. I told him to spend the time identifying how each individual was reacting to the change and then helping them move forward to help their teams. Then to keep doing it on a monthly basis.

After several months Brian told me that he had developed a system of spending 10 minutes per month with each of his people and they in turn spent 10 minutes with each of their factory people. He was beginning to notice the difference it was making and proudly stated that with one member of the team he had even spent 20 minutes!

When talking to people in organisations across all industry sectors, that are successfully managing change, one of the most common answers to the question, "What has made the greatest difference?" will be, "The behaviour of effective line-managers".

Could you spend a minimum of 10 minutes a month with each of your team, asking them how they feel about the change, putting to one side any conversations about tasks, projects, deadlines and actions? It will make a tremendous difference in terms of individual attention and addressing the underlying causes.

What if, all your direct reports who were people managers did the same thing? Just a relatively small amount of individual attention could save a large amount of time and money.

Think about your experiences of change in the past. Remember a time when you have received individual attention and someone has spent time helping you. If this has never happened, imagine it. It makes a difference.

"If speaking is silver, then listening is gold."
Turkish Proverb

7. Leadership Thinking – Change At An Organisational Level

So far we have considered ways in which you can help people at a team or individual level. Now I will introduce you to the Go MAD® Organisational Development Framework which is a powerful thinking tool for senior leadership teams who intend to implement large-scale changes in their organisations. The Organisational Development Framework is an adaptation of the original Go MAD® Thinking System and therefore has a direct read across to the principles and links.

You will remember the "hot cross bun diagram" on page 25 and the five organisational factors that are most likely to help or hinder a person's reaction to change that we introduced you to earlier. Investing in some time to apply this Framework to your leadership thinking will address all of the five organisational factors and will therefore pay back in terms of time and money saved in the long run.

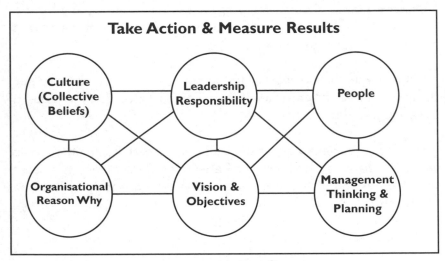

The Go MAD®
Organisational Development (O.D.) Framework

To help your leadership team with their thinking when planning or reviewing change there is a set of really useful questions based around the O.D. Framework that, if answered, will increase your probability of success. The key to these is to answer them as a leadership team – this will give you an opportunity to surface different perspectives and create an aligned team.

At the heart of the O.D. Framework is **Leadership Responsibility**. When using this model I recommend you start your thinking with this principle – if a change is going to be successfully implemented it is going to be the responsibility of the leadership team to put in place the infrastructure, processes and enablers, to manage both the task of change and people side of transition.

- What does leadership responsibility mean in this organisation and in the context of this change?
- How do/will we tangibly know when we are demonstrating leadership responsibility?
- What do we need to adopt or change in our behaviours as a leadership team to demonstrate a strong unified approach?
- How will we work as a team to help the organisation and each other move through transition?
- Are we prepared to take full responsibility for implementing this change?

Once you have absolute clarity on the leadership responsibility then as a leadership team you can ask questions based on the other five principles to help you both plan and review change.

Organisational Reason Why – this will stimulate your thinking around the internal and external drivers and motivators for change. Internal drivers might include: rising costs, poor workforce engagement, slow product innovation, restructuring, the need to replace out of date processes and equipment. External drivers might include: exchange rate fluctuations, increased competitor activity, legislative changes that require a different way of working, technological advances and environmental standards.

- What are the organisational reasons for change?
- What is the strongest reason for change?
- On a scale of 1 to 10 how passionate are we as a leadership team about making this change happen?
- Where would this change rank amongst our other priorities on a "reason why" scale?
- What processes could we put in during the change to check the strength of our organisational reason why?

Vision and Objectives – this principle allows you to test whether the organisational vision and objectives are expressed with absolute clarity and consistency and that the relevant people are able to describe it and buy in to it. In my experience it is not unusual for a set of individuals who make up a leadership team to have contrasting views on the vision and the timescale. This difference of opinion will have a knock on effect all the way down through the organisation.

- What is the leadership vision in relation to this change?
- How could we visibly communicate a consistent and aligned approach to the vision and objectives?
- How could we get clarity on exactly what it is we are going to do and by when?
- On a scale of 1 to 10 how achievable do we believe the vision to be?
- What steps could we put in place during the change to ensure we are still aligned and consistent and to check the vision and objectives are still relevant and achievable?

Culture – every individual holds a set of beliefs about themselves and their workplace. Those beliefs may be unchallenged assumptions and not necessarily facts and they may be engrained having been formed over many years. Regardless of the origin and validity of those beliefs, people will act in accordance with them. An organisational culture is the collective sum of your employees' beliefs (which can of course be either helpful or hindering), and the resulting behaviours.

- Will we achieve our vision with our existing culture?
- What will need to change and what will stay the same?
- How could we possibly champion, reward and role model the culture required, for change to occur?
- What hindering thoughts do we have as a leadership team that impact on our confidence to implement this change and what would be a more helpful thinking approach?
- How could we organisationally celebrate the small wins and successes along the way to help build the organisation's belief?

Management Thinking and Planning – this explores what management activity needs to take place to achieve the vision. This would include thinking about how much time managers are able to give to the achievement of the vision and to what extent their thinking and activities are in line with the organisational goals.

- How could we develop and equip managers with the style and skills to help their teams through transition?
- How much individual attention are we prepared to give to support those managers through their own transition?
- As a leadership team what could we do differently to release or create time for managers to enable them to focus on delivering the vision?
- How could we possibly communicate the vision and objectives for the change to this population in order that they have absolute clarity on their priorities and buy-in for the change?
- What could we do to develop solution focused thinking habits in this population?

People – paying attention to this principle will widen your leadership team's thinking about the range of people who need to be engaged and bought into the organisational goal, and the different strategies that might be required to involve them. This could include thinking about how you might segment employees into different "consumer groups" who may require different types and frequency of communication. For example, in your organisation there might be different leadership groups, different functional groups, and representative bodies such as the Trade Union.

As well as employees you could consider customers, shareholders, suppliers and other strategic partners or alliances.

- Who are the different people (either individuals or groups) that we need to communicate to and by when?
- How could we possibly communicate our vision for change in different ways to different groups?
- What responsibility will we take to ensure the change is communicated to others?
- How could we possibly find out what it is people want communication about and their preferred style of receiving information?
- Where and how could we get people involved at various stages of the change to reduce the feeling of powerlessness?

Take Action and Measure Results – using the Organisational Development Framework in change is not a one-off event. Make it part of your implementation and review processes as a diagnostic tool. Determine which principle needs the greatest attention and then act on it.

"Articulate the 'size of the prize' in a compelling way! To get the support of our entire workforce in one of our facilities, one of the key success factors was the way in which the reason for the change was articulated through face-to-face communication."
Chris Nex

TIME TO THINK

Q. What opportunities do you have in your business where applying the Go MAD® Organisational Development Framework would help improve the implementation of change?

Q. Using the framework as a diagnostic tool, which principles do you think need the greatest attention right now? (You could also refer to the questionnaire you completed earlier on pages 29-31 around the five organisational factors.)

Q. What actions will you take to strengthen or reinforce those principles that you have identified as needing attention?

8. Individual Thinking – Intended Actions

Start by understanding the effects of change on yourself.

Most individuals are influenced day-to-day by the people they see and communicate most frequently with. For many this will include their line-manager. If you are reacting against the change or struggling to accept it, then that message will be passed on to your people. This will happen, whether or not you are conscious of it, by the information you communicate, your tone of voice and body language. Hence, you can be of more help to others if you first help yourself.

Use the previous pages to help you consider the effects of change on yourself.

- Establish if any of the four underlying causes of a negative reaction to change apply.
- List the endings that the change has caused, or might cause you in the future.
- Locate your reaction to change on the Transition Curve.
- Analyse which of the five organisational factors hinder you most during change.
- Identify those things already determined and outside of your control (the givens).

Consider the three I's:

- What further information and explanation do you need?
- How involved do you feel? How could you become more involved?
- How much individual attention do you receive from your manager?
- How could you get a minimum of 10 minutes with them to talk about how you feel?

These last two questions are increasingly important the more senior you are in your organisation. Many senior managers and directors receive little individual attention from above. If this is the case, then external coaching and support might be an appropriate option.

"The significant problems we face cannot be solved at the same level of thinking we were at when we created them."
Albert Einstein

Notice your own thinking – is it helpful or hindering?

Do you talk to yourself about change in a mostly helpful or hindering way? Are you dwelling on the worry, uncertainty and potential problems? Hindering thinking only serves to hold you back from acceptance and moving forward.

Or are you focusing on resolving the challenges and realising the opportunities? Helpful thinking can move you forward.

As I said earlier – hindering thoughts are normal and natural. As you now have this knowledge and awareness of your own thinking, you can make a personal choice about whether you want to do something about it.

Here's the choice:

Hang on to your hindering thoughts and play them repetitively to yourself, (and potentially others) continually reinforcing all the worries and concerns that you have.

Or...

Choose to change the messages you play to yourself into more helpful, solution focused thoughts that move you forward.

If you choose the first option, recognise the possible risks and implications. For example, your own thinking will be recognised by your team and will therefore affect their own thinking. Hindering thoughts can be contagious! Also consider the impact of such self-talk on your own levels of performance, confidence and morale.

If you choose the second option then here is a four-stage process that you can apply to help yourself.

1. Increase your awareness of the messages you give yourself:
    - What are the sources or causes of the hindering thoughts?
    - Identify any common words, phrases or self-talk patterns.
    - Notice when you say these things to yourself.

2. Question any hindering thoughts about change:
    - To what extent are these really true or are they just assumptions or beliefs that you believe to be true but actually are not fact?
    - Is this way of thinking making you feel worse than you need to?
    - What is the long-term effect of taking this view of the change?

3. Consider more helpful ways of talking to yourself:
    - Focus on potential benefits.
    - How would you rather talk about change? What words would you benefit from replacing?
    - What could you do to see things differently? What would you need to do first?
    - What helpful thoughts do you already have about the changes that you could place more emphasis on?

4. Practise the new helpful self-talk:
    - Break out of a hindering self-talk vicious circle by consciously reprogramming your mind.
    - Catch yourself if the hindering self-talk surfaces. Consciously replace words and alter the messages you give yourself.

Whilst following this process may seem unnatural to start with, persevere with it until it becomes a habit. Major psychological studies have shown that people who are more helpful in the messages they give themselves are more successful in their ability to handle change.

Raise awareness and involve others

Consider your answers to the following questions and then decide your intended actions:

- How aware are other managers likely to be of "the secret" of managing change effectively?
- How skilful are other managers in helping individuals move through the transition process?
- What can you do to raise their awareness and ensure their skills are developed?
- Who else do you need to involve?

Key questions to ask at management meetings where change is being discussed or planned include:

- How will we involve people?
- How will we help people to adjust?
- How consistent is our management communication about the change?
- What will we do to help people move through transition?

Putting the "three I's" into regular and frequent practice makes good management sense, whether or not change is happening. The knowledge and skills covered in this book are common sense – yet, I also know that during change common sense and common practice are often two separate issues.

"Great leaders are almost always great simplifiers, who can cut through argument, debate, and doubt to offer a solution everybody can understand."
General Colin Powell

Put the secret into practice

There is little more to say other than go and do it. During the next few weeks, months and years you are likely to hear and talk about **change** many times. Hopefully that word will be a reminder of the **transition** that has to happen in order for change to be effective. Once reminded, commit yourself to take action to ensure it does happen.

Go MAD® (Make A Difference) about change in your organisation and reap the rewards of time and cost savings.

"I never worry about action, only inaction."
Winston Churchill

BULLET-POINT SUMMARY

The Necessary Knowledge:

- The difference between change (external) and transition (internal adjustment process).
- The "secret" – for change to be effective, transition has to happen.
- The four underlying causes of a negative reaction to change.
    - Sense of unfairness in the treatment of individuals.
    - Personal uncertainty and insecurity about the future.
    - Perceived powerlessness.
    - Resistance to the need to adapt to change.
- The three stages of adapting to change
  (Endings ⟶ Transition ⟶ Beginnings)
- The five organisational factors which have greatest impact on peoples' morale.
    - Clarity of future direction.
    - Senior management commitment to the change.
    - Individual perception of the planning and implementation of change.
    - Line management style and skills.
    - Communication.

The Essential Skills and Tasks:

- Address the underlying causes with the key management tasks (The Three I's)
    - Information and explanation
    - Involvement
    - Individual attention
- Help others accept the need for change by answering the five key questions.
    - What specific events brought about the change in our organisation?
    - Why was there a need to change?
    - Who was involved in the decision making process?

- What other options were considered and why were they rejected?
- What are the changes intended to achieve?
- Review the effectiveness of your written communication.
- Help people to identify endings.
- Apply the Go MAD® Thinking System to help you and your team with their thinking, before, during and after change.
- Use the Organisational Development Framework in your leadership team.

Intended Actions:

- Calculate the potential cost savings your organisation can make by successfully applying the secret of managing change.
- Understand the effects of change on yourself. Identify your own endings. Be a role model.
- Put the three I's into frequent practice with your people.
- Raise awareness of the people issues and transition at management meetings and with senior management.
- Remember that common sense is not common practice. It is easier to know than to do.
- Commit yourself to making a difference.

ABOUT THE AUTHORS

Andy Gilbert is the developer of the critically acclaimed Go MAD® Thinking System. He is passionate about helping people make a difference by developing their ability to think systemically in a solution focused way.

As Managing Director of Go MAD Thinking, Andy works worldwide designing business improvement programmes for organisations seeking to achieve results through transforming the way people think.

Author of over 100 books, video and audio programmes, he is a highly sought after public speaker and facilitator bringing his entrepreneurial flair and energy to a wide-range of businesses.

In addition to helping organisations save time and money by managing organisational change effectively, he specialises in helping individuals and organisations to make measurable differences through high impact leadership programmes.

Jo Hutchinson started her career in retail before moving into HR management with a variety of blue chip organisations across a number of industry sectors.

Now a Go MAD Thinking Engineer, Jo brings her experience and expertise to a range of leadership, change and business improvement programmes with a range of clients across the world.

An experienced senior leader, coach and facilitator of change, Jo has been able to help many individuals make a difference through her passionate advocacy of the Go MAD® Solution Focused Thinking approach.

ACKNOWLEDGEMENTS

In preparing this edition of the book we asked a few friends and clients for their words of wisdom in managing change based on their own personal experiences as leaders. A selection of these thoughts are shared with you in the form of quotations in this book, alongside quotations from more well known figures.

We would like to thank the following for making a difference with their contributions:

Jenny Briggs, Northampton General Hospital
Beth Chadwick, National Grid
Michael Gould, Hiscox Insurance
Judith Marples, Bradford College
Chris Nex, Rolls-Royce plc
Steve Ogle, Mercer Limited
Ben Reid, The Midcounties Co-operative
Keith Sparrow, DHL
Nicola Stout, McCann Erickson
Simon Wilson, Rolls-Royce plc

Has This Book Left You Wanting To Know More?

If you are seeking to make a difference within your organisation and would like to have a discussion about any aspect of applying Go MAD as a solution focused approach to leadership thinking, business improvement, coaching, management development or cultural change, then please contact us and a Go MAD Thinking Engineer will be happy to discuss possibilities.

Log on to www.gomadthinking.com to find out more about Andy, Jo and the Go MAD team and how they have been helping organisations to make a difference for over 10 years. Complete the personal thinking exercises to develop your own Solution Focused Thinking, sign up to our free e-zine and register for www.gomadthinking.tv – our online resource library.

Download and listen for free to our top ranked podcast series "Thinking for Business Success" on iTunes. Short, practical and entertaining, these cover many topics, including change and transition.

Contact us:
Go MAD Thinking
Pocket Gate Farm
Off Breakback Road
Woodhouse Eaves
Leicestershire
LE12 8RS
United Kingdom

t: +44 (0)1509 891313
f: +44 (0)1509 891582
e: info@gomadthinking.com
w: www.gomadthinking.com

Discover More Ways To Make A Difference

Our extensive resource and publications range is available from www.gomadthinking.com/shop or telephone +44 (0)1509 891313 to place an order.

Go MAD – The Art of Making A Difference
The original Go MAD personal effectiveness book and a great introduction to the Go MAD® Thinking System. (0-9543292-6-0)

Go MAD About Coaching + audio CD (via voucher)
Over 200 powerful coaching questions, plus tips, tools, techniques and templates. The manager's guide for helping others to make a difference. (0-9537284-8-X)

Go MAD About Negotiating
Achieving results through influencing the thinking of others. Practical easy-to-read case-studies and over 150 tips to consider when negotiating. (0-9551287-0-6)

Who's Driving Your Bus?
An inspirational story about the power of the Go MAD® Thinking System. (0-9537284-9-8)

59 Minutes to a Calmer Life
Practical strategies to help reduce stress in your professional and personal life. (0-9537284-3-9)

How to Save Time and Money By Managing Meetings Effectively
101 ways to lead meetings that create clearly defined outputs and engage people. (0-9543292-2-8)

How to Avoid the Training Trap
101 ways to ensure that development gives a great return on investment and really Makes A Difference. (0-9551287-3-0)

How to Make A Difference By Transforming Managers into Leaders
255 thought provoking tips to create passionate leaders who make a difference and love what they do. (0-9543292-3-6)

How to Win in Negotiations
130 tips for any one to adopt immediately in any negotiation to make a difference. (0-9543292-5-2)

How to Create a Culture of Commitment in Your Contact Centre
101 tips that will make your call centre a great place to work.
(0-9551287-3-0)

Why not sign up to our regular free ezine and receive a free ebook? Subscribe via www.gomadthinking.com.

Finally, if you are serious about your personal development and really want to make a difference as a leader in your organisation then contact us to discover more about the innovative Post Graduate Certificate, Diploma and Masters Degree qualifications we provide through Ashcroft International Business School in Cambridge.

NOTES/IDEAS

On this page, capture the ideas you have for making a difference in managing organisational change. Go on – see if you can get to 20!

1.

2.

3.

4.

5.

6.

7.

8.

9.

10.

11.

12.

13.

14.

15.

16.

17.

18.

19.

20.

NOTES/IDEAS

NOTES/IDEAS

NOTES/IDEAS